Hotel Raphael

RACHAEL BOAST was born in Bury St Edmunds in 1975 and has a PhD from the University of St Andrews. *Sidereal* (Picador, 2011) won the Forward Prize for Best First Collection and the Seamus Heaney Centre for Poetry Prize. *Pilgrim's Flower* (Picador, 2013) was shortlisted for the Griffin Prize. *Void Studies* (Picador, 2016) was shortlisted for the T. S. Eliot Prize. She lives in Bristol.

ALSO BY RACHAEL BOAST

Poetry

Sidereal

Pilgrim's Flower

Void Studies

Editor

The Echoing Gallery:
Bristol Poets and Art in the City
(Redcliffe Press)

The Caught Habits of Language:
An Entertainment for W.S. Graham
for Him Having Reached One Hundred
(Donut Press)

Rachael Boast

Hotel Raphael

PICADOR POETRY

First published 2021 by Picador
an imprint of Pan Macmillan
The Smithson, 6 Briset Street, London EC1M 5NR
EU representative: Macmillan Publishers Ireland Limited,
Mallard Lodge, Lansdowne Village, Dublin 4
Associated companies throughout the world
www.panmacmillan.com

ISBN 978-1-5290-3753-1

1 3 5 7 9 8 6 4 2

A CIP catalogue record for this book is available from the British Library.

Printed and bound by CPI Group (UK) Ltd, Croydon, CR0 4YY

FSC www.fsc.org
MIX
Paper from
responsible sources
FSC® C116313

עד־אנה

Ad-matai?

Book of Job, 19:2

Contents

I

II

Hotel Raphael

I

Hand, Match, Ashtray

We are sitting here to memorise the poem
before the pages I have wrapped myself in
are taken off, like a pleated dress, and burned
over an ashtray. The matches are there on the table.

This pain is not just our own, we have
a thousand hands, we are a forest of birches
outside the devastated city, tired of ordeals,
and of the tortured metal of icons we remain silent.

I mean to offer you the sound of bells ringing
from a faraway abandoned church, the smell
of scorched rafters and rubble, to say that fire
is also light. All this I saw in the mirror

and in the dream of the mirror your figure
hurrying across fields to a room with no walls
where the body is poem. We held each other
in that room and, for a moment, there was no pain.

Auspices

It's better not to move
in the long heat and languid evenings,
or maybe just this arm, looking
for a way of overcoming –

it will do its work. You bring
the silver breeze with you
up from the forest path, a delicate mercy
cool around my ankle like a bracelet.

Still I'm adorned with the fire
of the day. Don't fan the flames,
don't call the song thrush over
to beat her wings.

Gifts of the Weather Front

after Victor Erice

Today a Spanish plume will bring its trove of gifts
for the unwary, a wake-up call in the form of thunder
and a flash of night in an otherwise white sky,
the close air preceding it like a slow wave
that moves up from the south in a music box
containing only one note. I know this moment,
know it as a woman knows when something
breaks inside her. By dusk the sky will be red
and tomorrow will be clear, clear enough
to understand why things have to happen
in the order they happen according to the book
of the sky and the pages of the earth according
to the spine that keeps them all together.
And of that hinge Castilians still sing
healing gacelas, as in *O my dove, who art*
in the fissure of the rain-soaked rock
and in the secret places of abandoned buildings
or in the room where two children are sleeping
with a portrait of Tobias and the Angel
on the wall between them, the only waking thing.

The Diversion

He knew not what to do – Something, he felt must be done – he rose, drew his writing desk suddenly before him – sate down, took the pen – & found that he knew not what to do
– S.T. Coleridge, *Notebooks*

Scrambling down the fells
on a night walk lost for words
to describe the wilderness
between the peaks,
the wilderness of it all,
the ridges dropping in waterfalls,
the rocks themselves losing form
in the dark where mountains
become torrents turning
into lakes of skimming swallows,
the cottage swam into view.

What was said there no one will know;
the woman pouring tea,
her brother fetched from his bed
to hear the power of speech
at its most extraordinary –
a suspension of disbelief
written on the faces
lit by candlelight at an hour
that is neither night nor day –

then, disquiet silence,
falling back up the sides
of the fells in daylight witchery,
retracing steps taken only
a day or so ago, seeming now
so remote, his tongue sitting
in his mouth like a stone –
and he knew not what to do.

Brandy for bad dreams,
brimstone for burning pain,
poultices for swellings,
leeches to suck out the eyes
of boils: nothing was enough.

The stars moved around the sky
too rapidly, the landscape
changing as though centuries
were lost in a matter of days,
the fear of sleep leading
to a waking dream
in which fragments of speech
despise themselves and turn
against their speaker,
everything coming down
in deteriorating weather –
for he who, praying always,

prays in sleep unquietly,
prays again to rise from it.

He rose and drew his desk
towards him, ignored
the knocking at the door –
Gillman, Godwin
or Geraldine – ignored
the knocking in his head –
Ebon Ebon Thalud –
and knew not what to do
to stop the telescopic habit
of staring into his soul,
watching his own guiding star
crash into the eye of Antares.

Bitters for gout,
vinegar for nervous stress,
aquafortis for warts,
sal ammoniac for resurrection:
enough was enough,
for he who, praying always,
prays in sleep unquietly,
prays again to rise from it.

Mute

Switching the receiver to her other ear
with the thin cord around her neck she's not
on the phone to anyone talking of a yellow box
a yellow box in which she wants to put
the ashes of burned letters of sweet nothings
of blank photographs undeveloped and give them
back to no one as she lies down on the floor speaking
to no one cut off from the real world even as
the clock ticks and she lights another cigarette
waiting and waiting until she resumes her slow
octatonic ascent of language shifting between
the prevailing key and chromatic flashes of cold fury
that keep the door closed and the relationship
broken like a lock that can't be opened when no one
can help push her out of the room of the human voice
when it speaks without listening to the sound it makes
without the necessary aloneness and the heart
to ask herself who she is sitting there holding a pair
of driving gloves in her hand but not pulling them on
saying no, nothing, nothing, no, no, no darling, it's nothing.

Evening's Castle of Voices

(Hôtel Biron, 1911)

Those who, moving into their rooms,
sweep away the dust of disrepair
finding something written there
in the light that falls across the floor,
those who've chosen the right time
and place for a turning-point,
the hotel breathes them; its flourish
of steps leading to a lawn
where a party enjoys the *fêtes galantes*
of disturbing Venetian songs
floating over the heads of the wild roses
and brutal angels, unaware of the man
at his desk, in a high-backed chair,
whose possessions amount
to nothing as soon as he reaches
to grasp them; who no longer grasps
his own dimensions in that open room
where springtime doesn't need you,
where love means being alone.

Unfinished Admiration

Up in the woods on a level with the moon lifting
above the trees at the curve of the water
where the owls say *peut-être* with sharp tongues
having the wherewithal to continue exchanging
one side of the river for the other sounding out
the dark in a dialogue of place and displacement
as they come closer for a time playing safe
from a distance their proximate song, no longer
bothering with what hour or another has passed,
I'm looking for the poem which is sometimes
a place or a person or whatever immediately
makes the road a little brighter than it was before
with a sense of arrival – you at last, perhaps.

Disfigurations

John 5

How / do the narrators disagree over what light said about a stone?
– Mahmoud Darwish, 'In Jerusalem'

I

To a heap of stones broken from one stone;
to rubble, not without shape,

arid, not without something to say,
written in the dust, speaking, but not

with words; to a cairn considered
like this, all that is immovable in us

made into an offering to when the dust
of boundary stones becomes a road,

just as hours of grief create the need
for a journey, hours absolved by tears

that soften the stones of the road;
to the order of the journey and the stations

of rest; to the pool where the five porches
wait as a stranger troubles the waters.

II

I touch the back of my neck and feel grit,
a second skin that has no use other than

to make me a breach, and between
two separate ideas of normality I am

the tower with its embarrassment
of bells. I touch the face of rough metal

keeping it still, and then I push my luck.
It swings both ways until it finds a song

among all the other bells peeling away
the skin of the silence from the silence.

Lines Written in Provocation

You ask why am I here
where time has put me
here in the moment
of it answering the call
of two hands together
as one | and only after
the clap of the silent o'clock
(time doesn't like to be seen)
can I begin to ask why
I am here observing first
the room then the observing
of the room from my place
in time. Why am I here?
The moment draws in
its full breath | I am here
for certain only between
nuances of time that memory
works on, chiselling quartz
to make the hours
of aloneness lengthen.
Here I am. Where time
has put me to the test
of making something of it.
Let me see if I can make use
of it to answer – as it sounds
to my ear – your question.

Double Room

The way you last on me long after
our private minds like revolving doors
have led to a city hotel. It wouldn't matter
where, or when. Except for the need I'll have
for pots of hibiscus on either side
of the driveway. It could be Sharuhen
or Shaaraim. Anyhow, we'll know
where we are if the wallpaper
depicts a bluebird and a swallow
eating the eyes of the women of stone.
You'll call out Sophia or Sharon,
knowing full well I don't have a name.
We'll sleep soundly in the aromatic dream,
easily forgetting each other again.

The Infernal Method

'Enough! or Too much!'
– William Blake

It all boils down to a chalk seam,
duress of minerals, the wrong kind of rain.
Jupiter gives, Saturn takes away.
Your aggravated skin grows at a rate
envied by the best amphibious relative –
salamander or frog, eyes popping
into fresh sockets, the lizard bingeing
on its own calcium deposits, sometimes
in pieces and sometimes in one piece.
You walk along St Swithun Street
signalling nonchalance, a need not
to have to explain the inexplicable hell
of circles, and then loop back to a bench
by the cathedral, hoping no one's noticed
the colours of ordeal, the hot and dry
cartography of scars. To no avail. Start again.
You're learning the infernal method:
how to treat fire with fire, if all else fails;
a caustic pilgrimage 'salutary and medicinal,
melting apparent surfaces away' – except
it doesn't. Stop. Start again. Jupiter gives,
Saturn takes away. You continue along
the perimeter wall by the Itchen river,

her green curtains closed. How to hold fire
and keep moving? Fire on fire, cancelling
itself out. And round again, assuming
a measured pace as you pass back
through the city gate to College Street
where a fine dust spreads over the books
in P&G Wells and you pull out a copy
of *Answer to Job* with the god-awful
cheese grater on the cover,
sliding it back into its capable abyss.
Jupiter gives, Saturn takes away everything
except for the catastrophic weather of skin.

Tobias in the Fountain

In days of heat the water iris falls open
in the fountain next to the boy

standing up to his ankles, his thighs
and groin soaked to darken the stone

of selfhood with an endless stream
pushing through him and out

of the mouth of the fish swept up
in his arms. There is no sign of a struggle,

none at all. The water pours. The fish,
in giving its life to the boy, is twice alive,

like it or not. Like it or not, I sit
as near as I can to the absconding drops.

Ablutions for Midsummer

Over and over the moon washes her fragments
in the water, moving downstream as she does so,
following the foxglove wall to where yesterday
I walked on, seeing what I hadn't seen, hearing
what I hadn't heard, alert to the stresses
falling into water-paths excited by stone,
echoing the above into the below
as they move towards the hinge of the valley,
the river in spate, page after page turning
on a rhyme, repeating the word *water*
over and over again. Over and over again
the moon washes her fragments in the water
moving downstream as she does so, following
the foxglove wall to where the dark wood
listens into itself. A slab of cloud holds
in the shape of an anvil hammered by nothing
into nothing. My mind is bracken, catching
the flying sparks of rain over and over again.
The moon washes her fragments in the water
but this doesn't last. I'm glad it doesn't last.
How else could I come back to this house
on the rock overlooking the moor, listening
to long waves of air releasing another shower
from the speaking leaves of the wood?

To the Chief Rearranger of Raindrops

Tonight all the stars are falling,
all the falling lucky stars of rain at once
a happiness and necessary psalm of tears.
It will happen again, given our bodies
are alert to changes in the weather
and at times must curl in fear of the storm
of our near-enemies. But sit here
at my right hand. I've taken off my clothes,
am standing outside, laughing
as the downpour softens my skin
and The Whole Heaven in Your Eyes
falls on my face, tincture for this
ancient duress, your speaking fingers
pressed to the living moment of my lips.

Ichthyosis

Up against the wall you feel
for the door along endless years

of wall. Sometimes it's there
or disappears. Always the way

is through to the same thing
over. A wall, another door,

a few years on. The same again.
The act itself becomes mystery

then art. Each wall and each door
composes itself for your arrival.

It Never Crossed my Mind

[T]he wind will carry away their remains, and their achievements
will be given over to the storm wind
– 'Advice to a Prince'

In the new dispensation, we did ask
a member of the government to come on
the programme but no one was available.
We did ask a member of the government
to come on the programme but no one
was made available. We did ask the government
to talk to us but they didn't want to.
We did ask the government to join us tonight
but they declined to do so. We did ask
the government to respond but they said no.
Peace did not break out across the party ranks
or among the angelic orders. And so
if the advisor or the chief officer decrees
hostility on the judges of the land, the land
will fail and the queen of destinies
will cover their houses in shame.
If you inscribe a treaty void to levy
favourable winds, the northern walls
of the kingdom will shatter. In light of this,
the committee has met for breakfast.
Someone proffered anchovies and vodka.
Someone had nothing to offer. Someone

was polishing a knife. The chief officer
speaks from the same forlorn rose garden.
Listening is salutary, so pay attention
to your distraction. (God speed o fly,
heavenly sign, god speed star of the show,
wiping your feet on timely denial.)
Naturally, the topiary provides no solution
and in seasonal passage we cover our faces,
in loud weather, in a land without leaders.
Retrograde to 700 BC. Peace did not
break out across the party ranks
or among the angelic orders, who refused
to be interviewed. Instead, the oracle
speaks through her fog of chemicals.
The greenness of water hosts a clean signal
when the trees are singing, the air is singing,
and everything is in the balance.
Lamentation echoes across cities,
in the mirrors of hallways, in absentia.
Step away from the door. Tyrants always fall.

Room Service

The difficulty of being at the Welcome
is having two rooms on the go –
room twenty-two for breakfast juice
and enduring the police patrol
and room twenty-three for the work
of waking dreams and the mysteries
of the birdman. Here the windows
remain closed for the self-portraiture
that comes of wrestling with angels –
flashbacks of young Heurtebise
writing at the desk in the rue d'Anjou
now taking on horrific proportions,
one wing folded behind his neck,
the other cruel with razor-sharp
grimaces. The walls have eyes, lodged
from a past of the litanies of pilgrims.
Nothing much has changed –
time alternates, prostration to agitation,
mind and body suffering in the sun,
life dragging on through *nigredo*,
dark night of the soul, outer blackness
and the blackness within consuming
all poisons, all ecstasies, all forms of love.

Misprint

after Andrei Tarkovsky

The green and blue distance
bending slightly as she sits
on the fence rebalancing
the hours spent measuring
time by apparitions there
at the edge of the silent field
relenting into the space
between where she is
and who she will become
in a vision of walking towards
the mirror to see her hair
has turned grey in the black
and white room of rain
falling through the falling
ceiling all those years later
searching for the fateful word
with nothing to hold to
but the sound of her shoes
echoing along the corridor
becoming the stresses of the lines
of a lament for delayed light
for words that will not stop
and can't be wiped away.

Gathering the Wood

White blossoms faint on drafts of air
sweep the blue floor of the ancient wood.
My hands have become like wood,

gathering these branches and logs
leaning their dry gravity against
the tree, all of it in the balance of the rest.

No one knowing where I am
where no one passes on the high slope
I have made a place to camouflage myself,

to hold language over what is most
keenly unsaid. Songs in the carriages
of the wind ride over my head.

Ariel Head of the River

I sit down to gather myself
upstairs in the old boathouse
where everything is broken,
the signage loose from its bolt
swaying from the rusted veranda.
I'm trespassing again.
I need to hear myself think
next to the long mirror
of whatever moves with zero
velocity and gets to where
it needs to be in dry weather.
I'm looking for the slowness
with which things fall apart,
the poem which cannot be written
anywhere but in the dust
of disuse, in derelict light,
at a table I imagine to be here.
The low vibrato of an owl
fills the room which is neither
out nor in. I swing on my chair
conducting this chaos
of images rhyming internally
with the things of the world
to contest their separateness,
while time like the grey rag
of a bird stands in the shallows,
feet relaxed in mud;

the escapade of living rings
she leaves behind collapses
into its own. I watch them go.
I am smoothed over, a moment
in a mirror continuing to survive.

II

Testament

(November 1918)

From Apollinaire's star-shaped head wound
grew your signature, flower of shrapnel,
mercurial flower, the fatal hurt

of a moment's fire bursting into life –
for such is art, such is the calligram
of its five petals of resistance seeping

into the edge of an age to indicate
that sometimes, instead of closing,
the wound stays open and speaks.

The star continues turning itself
into a flower, the flower into testimonies
of distance such as those that remain

when others leave us, or never arrive –
star that doesn't know the meaning
of goodbye, only *see you*, or *night sky*

Open Book

(London, 2011)

The smog thickens towards nightfall.
Let Akhmatova walk with me
as far as the corner.
A choir of discord is growing
in the city. All the stores
are open late, everything
under lock and key displaced
as the noise increases,
the air crackling with static,
with slogan, the Party HQ
billowing smoke from its doorway.
I wipe my eyes and step
into the shattered road.
'Here? Is this the place?'
Nothing has been touched.
I wasn't to know that whoever
presses their face to the glass
will see themselves become sylvan
through an uncommon visage.
A decorated tree is flourishing,
pushing up from under the floor,
ancient and inevitable.
A book slips from its purchase
in the branches, falling open

at a page on which is written
the language of a silent cache
where time has not been passing.

Silent Sea

(Paris, 2015)

We were the first that ever burst
Into that silent sea
– S. T. Coleridge

Another vessel sheds the chrome
of its silver mile until a mile
meanders into three, triples again

over the reef. Nothing can breathe
under oil, nor register that
dark membrane's slick

over sight. *We were the first*
cracking the hull of the earth
open, our foolish husbandry

a metallurgy that's brimmed
with false gold too often
we can talk and talk and talk

but on a ship in space, manned
by *non-thinking from non-feeling,*
we say absolutely nothing at all.

Art^2

(on *Chatterton* by Henry Wallis)

For the sake of art
I praised the metals
that purged me.
Thank fuck for Zarnikh!
Etcetera. Etcetera.

O parapets!
My porches of deed and word.
The walls I was up against!
Art as a verb. My beingness!
Not this!

A tinsel-haired fetch
pretending to be me
when, like Christ,
I was in two places
at once, admiring
the trove of buried languages
only to pull out
my posthumous assessment
of your appalling depiction
of my death.

O Meredith!
Tyme nowe you mov'd alonge
for Mary Ellen has gon!

Ill-treated in life
and in art, here I am,
backlit, posed as pietà,
a stage-managed non-being.
Not I.

I haunt this room in the form
of a pulled back
curtain. I am
the window and the view!
I am the plume of violet smoke,
the one rose.
I am all colours
and I am not, Meredith,
there at all!

O gargoyles!
My porches of lust and word.
And look what befalls those
who assume they know my pain,
passing it off
with a pissy flourish.

O Meredith!
Tyme nowe you mov'd alonge
for Mary Ellen has gon!

[2] /aːrt/ archaic or dialect second person singular present of be: *I am a Gentleman as thou art not.*

Dark Saying

In ancient tales of ordeal
protagonists were urged
to inhabit a place of rival
certainties: with their backs
against a wall maybe,
or blind between two pillars,
or sitting on an ash heap,
the body wincing in its wrapper.
I move the scene to the edge
of a river – the Tigris
or Jordan. Here they are,
kneeling in an attitude
of supplication. Who wins,
the one bending to drink
straight from the source,
or one who cups their hands?
The cradle of civilisation
has been broken. The farmers
protest in the city square.
The rivers of the world
run dry. Over and above,
the moon looks and looks, says
don't call me priestess of grief –
what you've been searching for
is not in this silver box

Timbre

I

The air of the road perpetuates
the singalong of last night's visit,
Patrick, hours brimming with the snow
of carbonated gold. The monotone
white sky requires some examination
but the pet names of Socrates escape me
if, in this deafness of being half in
and half out of the day, it matters.
What did I tell you? In the cabinet of noon
life is crystal to my licked finger.
Aye, here's the rub, I'm glad to hear
you got home by raising your voice
like a head-torch along the good road.

II

The ringing of crystal perpetuates
the singalong of the night road
a few days on. I'm drunk with this
sound in my ears of waves reading
a drowned volume falling through
the depths of a lagoon somewhere
off the map. Here is a leaf taken
from that book to help to keep me
pedalling these words against the air.
What moves without sound? What
with? Something legless and alive
in the saying of it relays the din
of this underwater ordnance.

III

The road of canticles perpetuates
the singalong that suggests
I could do a proper Berryman
on this tinnitus. So much mileage
to the road I'm walking down
less alone in this bone cloud
and closer to what matters.
Lend me your ear, tuned to the hum
I've turned into, this receptacle
that longs for the waters of home
until water is all that it knows.
Malleus and Nimbus construct
this wrought prayer house.

External Line

Here we are, silent for a moment
between the words. I'm in
the other room on the telephone,
hearing the telephone ringing
from the room you have landed in,
falling through the ceiling
from whatever shaped cloud
has carried you. Pick up the receiver.
Careful how you answer so the line
doesn't break . . . are you there?
Here I am in my ice palace
under the white sheet where only
the language of your evening eyes
will keep the cold prologues
from freezing over. I wanted
to say more about the line
before giving you directions
to the desk where I'm sitting
with my breath visible in front
of my face, how syntax is the weather
and can alter the weather
which in a second will change.
Your room is made up from the light
inside a thunderclap. Now
go through the double doors
at the end of the hall, and on and on
and through the door beyond that.

I'll turn around to see the shadow
of your form on the paper-thin wall.
I'm here with you only to pull
your full figure of speech towards me.

Passing Through

Dr Blackall's carriage tears around Brake Corner
en route to the highest point as the stars appear.

I've lost track of time, and so has he, it being
hard to say if the hour is such and such or not

on a night as wide as this one is, the loose stones
of words rolling sharply under the wheels of time.

He and I are sound and vista, in memory
of prayer and sanctuary – two hands together

rubbing along. I talk too much while he looks out
across the moor at the various upheavals.

Let's say it might be three fifteen, or five past one.
We pass through our lives in a flicker of habitation.

How did he turn that corner? He lights his wood pipe
ahead of Mel Tor, holding fast its house of bees.

Seven Protections

Protection by Beech trees, their roots
watered with wine, their leaves
a glossary of rhyming words.

Protection by Birch, the white lady
of the woods, her sky-ladder
intensified by winter dreams.

Protection by Quicken Tree, the red one,
holding its oracular branches
to draw yourself up and over the wall.

Touch wood. Pick up sticks
for locating metal, water, boundaries,
paths that take you up again.

Protection by the broad Oak, who speaks
slowly, rustling his messages
as the sun opens a door into the hillside.

Protection from sleeplessness,
tap-tap-tap the saplings of Holly divine
this dream-like stepping. Then up again.

Protection by eating the cold air
blowing across hieroglyphic bracken,
the book of the land lying open.

‘That one and only hour’

All for nothing a feather floats backwards
surfaces appear of white and pink extremities

of blossom and wings. Across this line
and the next of the tide moving towards me

as emissary of light fragmented by movement
I remember your face as a river of looking.

Tear and mend me, currently. Be here again
waiting to embark or as a wind speaking

on the water, either way. No one else can.
I gather up the erratic play of sparks

and throw them back in to ask the question
I asked before as to when and where this was

Leaves of Maria the Shepherdess

What an effort at life, this tree
under which the poem lives,
under which I have placed
a blue chair. Her leaves
press down the notes
of the water. The silence
is silver. I can't stop looking
to belong to the nation
of small things. Falling leaves.
Broken surface. Salvia in excelsis.
Maria, Maria – the door
of your wings is disintegrating.

Winter Rose

There being nothing to look at
on the white page but for this
pressing weight, and something
that flowers in the deficit,
where to begin feathering
the emptiness from which I can
survey my limits? These late hours
are a cold medley of petals
on a rose stubbornly open
beyond its season, unspeakable,
like the terrible work of God's mercy.
There being nothing to add
and nothing as read, life keeps
moving in me like a childlessness.
My future, my lifeline in another
form withheld. Instead I create
conditions in which to thrive,
albeit in a time like ours when
to sing is easier than speaking.
There's danger in the setting
down of the unsettled ultimately
failing to fill this need. I want
to lift you up and hold you.
Song takes precedence again,
left to age and seep through any
dilemma, the pink breath of song
defrosting the tongues of winter.

Souvenir

A book left open on a glass balcony
overlooking terraces of wild country,
leaves turning randomly by themselves
next to a half-empty cup of coffee.

Who is the author of these pages,
the frontispiece giving way to a series
of rapid quatrains, reading and re-reading
the landscape, the wind coming over the hills?

Moment in a Labyrinth of Moving Images

after Alain Resnais

You know this place, the hotel where voices
go missing down baroque corridors
leading nowhere, and then to the mirror,

then back to her. Proportions of place
and personage form an hourglass
by cutting from one man picking up shards

off the black and white tiles to another laying
cards down on the table. Shuffle the sands
of time. She doesn't like to talk at night.

Sentences frozen in space resume elsewhere.
You know this place, the hotel where voices
go missing down baroque corridors leading

nowhere and then to the mirror. Then back
to her. She doesn't move from her chair.
Why does she not move from her chair?

As ever, no one will answer with an answer
to the question that's been asked but to another
that hasn't. What was it? You know this question.

A rhyming shot in expression and decor,
in evening dress. You are obsessed
by absence, drawing her near with hours

of conversation in a void. You know this place,
an epic simile in one mirror after another
then back to her, then nowhere, time and again.

Across the Listening Void

Beside each other perched
On the Epidaurus steps
– W. S. Graham

I found the door you left on the page
and turned its key, stepping into the words,
noting each print on the white field holds
the sound of the moment it was made,

holds the slow pace of how time sings
a life to a life across the listening void.
My ears are full of the silence of snow
melting on the moor, of mist in the trees

hanging with all the other works of art
that occur by themselves while I make
these sounds like tins to ring out

and say, well now, here is the door
you left open on the page which
holds the key to the printed field.

Belle Époque

What we're given is a sidelong view of her, you say,
meaning a view through the eyes of another

in a chapter of a memoir, but what I see is a woman
on a couch with raven hair tied back in contrast

to the length of her limbs and the space allowed
those long fingers softly abstracting into the white

of the canvas to become completely relaxed,
as is the neck and face, the attitude of the times,

the growing need for her Parisian visits, the roses
appearing on the floor so perfectly on the day

the studio was locked by mistake, the elegance
of the line from then on, each subject elongated

in the reach that desire makes towards its ideal,
reaching back to Anna, always Anna, silent woman

with a memory that holds like ice the poems
of the Neva, moving on through small joys

and terror until the thaw, I say, looking over
at your profile, your hand turning the yellowed page.

Vertical Gardens

This could be any city in one lifetime or another,
at a hotel we've never been to, at the Square
which could be the Square of Pegasus

where the Lady Inanna sings her dark songs
to a slide guitar in a language unheard,
in a time not yet ours. I've been waiting

for this moment beyond the moment
where I'm waiting for the waiting to end
as we try not to look over at each other,

except from the corner of our eyes,
for it's not that the room we're in is too bright
but that we see the light that lives inside

our looking, within which vines and creepers
of scented flowers cover a gate made of cedar
and wrought iron in the shape of thoughts

that can't be spoken – but somehow it opens –
and we find ourselves on the roof of a ziggurat
where offerings have been left for centuries

or more, the sides and the stairways covered
in foliage, turned into vertical gardens
for the god of the star of planetary strife

and the star of the life-giving water
and the word. We see it all in a blink,
drawn back to the room where the lady still sings

of the sanctum that cannot be entered
except in moments like this, when heaven
is left hanging in the underworld.

Now let's wake from this verdant dream,
and let the early hours heal us, having drunk
the ordeal poison from the poisoned stream.

On Simplification

These words come easily into their meaning now,
a fragrant hand that opens out the residue

that the years come down to, the crushed
lavender picked from the steps leading up

to your house, or to where you are now.
Life fades into the full flower of the dark.

The gift of the dead is the remembrance due,
your hand reaching out, just as it used to,

for the matches laying there on the table,
for lighting, one more time, the sleeping candle.

On Confession

The waters are hid as with a stone
– Job 38:30

I wouldn't want to put it down in writing
but perhaps, in a speak easy way, confess
to a pleasure for how a porous host
exaggerates its bitters. An ozone smell
of weather fronts released into static air
isn't giving much away as summer presents
herself for stormy inspection. Meanwhile,
in the Land of Uz, anxiety is impersonal.
The corporeal dress of our lady of sorrows
embroidered with everything under the sun
carries this advice to leaders tucked in its hem:
If you heed a rogue, Nābû, who organises
heaven and earth, who directs all things,
will throw your people into chaos
and your land will be devastated.
Which is fair enough. But who are we now,
walking the night-vaulted corridors
of the Hôtel–Dieu, looking for our twin,
knowing that where we wake up depends
on how we dream? Here, signals and laughter
hang in the willows that herald the dawn.
Over there, arrears of vesper and winter.

St Raphael's on the Moor

Down along the trail where the course
of the water and the path are confluent
over the loose stones given the voice
of a singing path that saves me
from thinking, I'm somewhere
between setting out and arriving.
I wash my face in its vowels.
I soak my eyes with its momentary silver
and carry on, over the black and white
glissando in fragments of granite
until the road passes between there
and there-over, into a prayer house,
the double doors painted blue,
the scrape of oak across flagstone,
the late hour's holding back
of the bell of tears. What a world –
how it swings between this and that,
how it calls and calls. At the end
of the pews, white quills to match
the white walls with arched wings
of silent stone waiting for me to write
something. But my words come out
altered, lifted into this after-place
of what can be relied on. I fold this
message up into my stepping out
to take the path back into the wood.

READING | VIEWING

'Hand, Match, Ashtray': cf. Lydia Chukovskaya, *The Akhmatova Journals, Volume I* (Harvill, 1994) | 'Gifts of the Weather Front': cf. *The Spirit of the Beehive* (dir. Victor Erice, 1973) | 'The Diversion': 'Edon Edon Thalud' is a reference to the druggist in *1001 Nights* | 'Mute': based on Jean Cocteau's *La voix humaine* as performed by Ingrid Bergman | 'Evening's Castle of Voices': the last line uses a phrase from Rainer Maria Rilke's 'Requiem for a Friend'. Set in the Hôtel Biron (now the Musée Rodin), one of the figures on the lawn is Jean Cocteau, who never met Rilke although they were both living there at the same time. cf. Francis Steegmuller, *Cocteau: A Biography* (Macmillan, 1970) | 'Lines Written in Provocation': written from a prompt – "Why am I here?" – from a narration by W. S. Graham in a BBC Monitor arts programme, *Why Cornwall?* | 'To the Chief Rearranger of Raindrops': cf. Psalm 110 | 'It Never Crossed my Mind': cf. 'Advice to a Prince' in *Babylonian Wisdom Literature*, ed. W. G. Lambert (Oxford University Press, 1960) | 'Room Service': Cocteau at the Welcome Hôtel, cf. Steegmuller, *Cocteau: A Biography* | 'Misprint': cf. *Mirror* (dir. Andrei Tarkovsky, 1975) | 'Ariel Head of the River': for a discussion of the meaning of the word 'Ariel' see Samuel Feigin, 'The Meaning of Ariel', in *Journal of Biblical Literature*, Vol. 39, No. 3/4 (Society of Biblical Literature, 1920) | 'Open Book': draws from Anna Akhmatova's 'The Way of All the Earth' (in a translation by Peter Norman) and is a response to the unrest in London during August 2011 | 'Silent Sea': cf. *Coleridge's Notebooks, A Selection*, ed. Seamus Perry (Oxford University

Press, 2002) | 'That one and only hour': takes its title from a line in Ciaran Carson's 'Fée', from *In the Light Of* (Gallery Press, 2012) | 'Moment in a Labyrinth of Moving Images': cf. *Last Year at Marienbad* (dir. Alain Resnais, 1961) | 'Belle Époque': on Akhmatova's encounter with Amedeo Modigliani. cf. Anna Akhmatova, *My Half Century*, Selected Prose, ed. Ronald Meyer (Ardis, 1992) | 'On Confession': adapts lines from 'Advice to a Prince' and uses a phrase from Carolyn Forché's *The Angel of History* (Bloodaxe, 1994).

ACKNOWLEDGEMENTS

Thanks to the editors of the following publications in which some of these poems, or versions of them, first appeared: *1914 Poetry Remembers* (Faber, 2013), *Bad Lillies, Chicago Review, Festival of the Future City* (Bristol Cultural Development Partnership, 2015), *Guardian, Magma Poetry, Off the Shelf: A Celebration of Bookshops in Verse* (Picador, 2016), *Poetry, Poetry Ireland Review, Poetry London, The Poetry Review, Prac Crit, Stand, The Scores, Try to be Better* (Prototype, 2019) | 'The Diversion', based on 'Christabel' being rejected from *Lyrical Ballads* volume two, was commissioned for the Bristol Festival of Ideas, 'A New Lyrical Ballads' | 'Mute' was commissioned for *The Verb* as part of the BBC's Classical Voice season | 'Testament' was commissioned to mark the centenary of the start of the First World War | 'Silent Sea' was commissioned for the *Guardian*'s 'Keep it in the Ground' Climate Change Campaign and set to music by Sally Lamb McCune for the Judith Clurman Choral Series, published by Hal Leonard | 'Art^2' was commissioned for Lyra Festival and the Bristol Cultural Development Partnership as part of 'A Poetic City', supported by the National Lottery Heritage Fund | 'Timbre' is dedicated to Patrick Brandon | 'External Line' was commissioned and recorded for 'Dial-a-Poem', a multimedia community project supported by the AHRC and Nottingham Trent University | 'Passing Through': i.m. Ciaran Carson | 'Across the Listening Void' was commissioned for BBC Radio 3's *The Verb* for a programme celebrating the centenary of W. S. Graham | 'Belle Époque' won the 2015 Bristol Poetry Prize | 'Vertical Gardens' was commissioned for the Bristol Festival of Ideas, 'Festival of the Future City' | 'On Simplification': i.m. Sheila Zurbrugg | Thanks are due to the Society of Authors and Arts Council England for financial assistance | Grateful thanks to the Royal Literary Fund for their invaluable support | With love and gratitude to Annie Freud, Don Paterson and my three Eagle Rock hosts, Rupert Lane, Petra Tilly and Woodruff | Special thanks to Andy Ching to whom this book is dedicated.